T0040294

THE PROTEIN SMOOTHIE BIBLE

THE PROTEIN SMOOTHIE BIBLE

FUEL YOUR BODY, ENERGIZE YOUR LIFE, AND LOSE WEIGHT

ERIN INDAHL-FINK

Skyhorse Publishing

Copyright © 2019 by Erin Indahl-Fink

All rights reserved. No part of this book may be reproduced in any manner without the express written consent of the publisher, except in the case of brief excerpts in critical reviews or articles. All inquiries should be addressed to Skyhorse Publishing, 307 West 36th Street, 11th Floor, New York, NY 10018.

Skyhorse Publishing books may be purchased in bulk at special discounts for sales promotion, corporate gifts, fund-raising, or educational purposes. Special editions can also be created to specifications. For details, contact the Special Sales Department, Skyhorse Publishing, 307 West 36th Street, 11th Floor, New York, NY 10018 or info@skyhorsepublishing.com.

Skyhorse® and Skyhorse Publishing® are registered trademarks of Skyhorse Publishing, Inc.®, a Delaware corporation.

Visit our website at www.skyhorsepublishing.com.

10 9 8 7 6 5 4 3

Library of Congress Cataloging-in-Publication Data is available on file.

Cover design by Qualcom
Cover photo credit: Erin Indahl-Fink

Print ISBN: 978-1-5107-4216-1
Ebook ISBN: 978-1-5107-4217-8

Printed in China

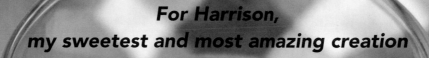

For Harrison,
my sweetest and most amazing creation

Contents

Introduction

Hello, my name is Erin and I'm the author of *The Protein Smoothie Bible*. I'm a happily busy mom, wife, food writer, photographer, and small business owner doing my best to juggle multiple balls in the air all at once. Just like many, I'm trying to balance my kids' school and activities schedule, doing my best to be as productive as possible with my work, be the best wife and partner, and oh, yeah . . . that self-care thing. At the end of the day, things are typically taken care of, but what gets sacrificed the most is my diet. Can you relate?

I wrote this book to provide you, me, and everyone else who struggles with making the best diet choices to have some simple, healthy options to fuel our bodies. Often, the hardest part about making healthy food choices is just knowing *what* to choose. These recipes are designed to be especially simple and easy to make. Easy breakfast, lunch, or snack ideas that you can see yourself making and enjoying! Amazing, right?!

The recipes in this book have been written to be very approachable. I've specifically chosen ingredients in each recipe to be found by as many people as possible. Growing up in rural America, we had fruits and vegetables but were sometimes limited by seasonality or availability. I didn't try papaya, or for that matter even knew what it was, until I was twenty-five. Every recipe in this book will contain easy-to-find, un-weird ingredients that everyone has access to, despite geography or economic status. Good food should be available to us all—not just some of us.

My goal for us and this book is to inspire your own personal healthy living. I want you to open this book and see that, "Hey, I can totally do this!" or "This recipe looks easy, and it will help me enjoy more vegetables!" If this book inspires you to try just one new fruit or vegetable or blend up something that you would have never otherwise thought of, then that's outstanding! Sometimes living our best life means living the life that brings us the most joy, the most happiness, and the most health.

Cheers to joy, happiness, and health!

Erin

Chapter 1
Prepping for Success

WHY SHOULD YOU MAKE YOUR OWN SMOOTHIES?

Just about every fast-food joint, coffee shop, and fancy grocery store will happily blend up a smoothie, Frappuccino, or shake of your choosing. But do you know what is in that drink? Do you have an idea of all the products they are including in that beverage? If not, maybe you should consider making your own.

Here are just a few benefits of blending your own smoothies:

1. **You control the ingredients you're consuming.**

   When blending your own smoothies, you can control the ingredients and amount that you want to consume. You'll be able to regulate the flavors with real, simple ingredients. When using fruits, vegetables, nuts, and proteins, the nutrition will be enhanced and coming from significant sources.

2. **You control the sugar.**

   When making your own smoothie, you're able to have full control of the amount of sugar or choice of sweetener included in your drink. Often fast-food/store-bought smoothies are upwards of 60 grams of sugar. Would you still consider this a healthy option for a snack, breakfast, or meal? A little later we'll talk about choosing the best sweetener for your smoothie.

3. **It will save you money.**

   You can blend a better, more flavorful smoothie for much less than it costs to buy one at a drive-thru or fancy retailer. Who doesn't want a little extra green in their pocket at the end of the day?

4. **It will save you time.**
   The average recipe in this cookbook takes just five minutes to make, from start to finish. Think of the time you spend driving, waiting in line, and waiting for your retail drink to be made. It's likely more than five minutes.

Begin keeping some basic ingredients in your refrigerator, freezer, and pantry. You likely already have some of the basics. You'll be able to provide yourself and your family with healthier, flavorful, and satisfying breakfasts, snacks, and lunches with just a few simple steps. These protein smoothies will fuel your body and energize your day so much more than any expensive, over-sugared, store-bought drink.

LET'S TALK ABOUT INGREDIENTS

CHOOSING YOUR PROTEIN AND MAKING SUBSTITUTIONS

As I mentioned in the introduction, each smoothie is specifically designed to be easy to make and include a reasonable amount of protein. However, some of you may have specific dietary restrictions, preferences, and allergies. Here are some great substitution options that will help customize your smoothie to your dietary needs.

DAIRY & LACTOSE INTOLERANT

Steer clear of any yogurts and animal milks as you usually do. Your protein options are vast, including soy, plant-based, or collagen protein powders. You can also add nuts and seeds along with nut and seed butters to your smoothies. As always, make sure to read labels to ensure you're choosing the best possible protein for your nutritional needs.

NUT ALLERGIES

Protein powders (soy, whey, plant-based or collagen) along with Greek yogurts will be your BFFs! As always, make sure to read labels and choose products that best fit your nutritional needs. Cottage cheese is also a high-protein option, should you want to give it a try.

PROTEIN POWDER ADVERSE

Nuts and seeds, along with nut and seed butters and yogurts, will be your primary sources of protein. There are some wonderfully nutritious protein sources, just be sure to watch labels for any processed sugar. Yogurts are notorious for adding extra sugar. Plain Greek yogurt is always a great option when trying to steer clear of sugar. It's high in protein and you can add your own sweetener as needed. Additionally, cottage cheese is another high-protein alternative.

VEGAN FRIENDLY

Plant-based proteins will be your best friends. There are more and more plant-based protein powders coming onto the market every day. Choose one that best fits your nutritional needs and tastes. Don't hold back on the nuts, seeds, and nut butters. As always, read your labels and select products that best fit you, and make sure to keep an eye out for unnecessary refined sugars.

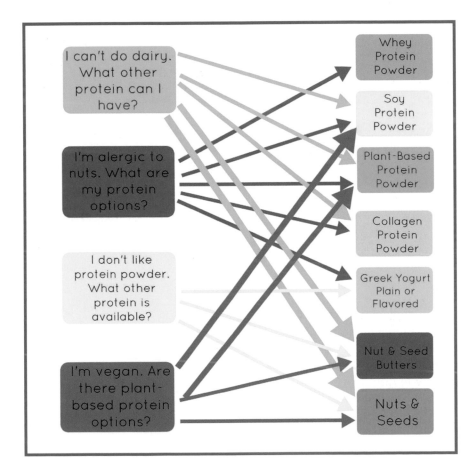

PROTEINS TO AVOID IN SMOOTHIES

It likely goes without saying, but I'll say it anyway—raw meat, eggs, seafood, and shellfish are not recommended in a smoothie. Not only are there food safety issues, but including these ingredients in a smoothie may not taste great either. Save your meats, eggs, and fish for other meals. I'm all about a great steak or scrambled eggs when cooked and seasoned to perfection.

MILK CHOICES

Dairy, cashew, almond, soy, coconut, rice, and many more! There are now more milk options on the market than ever before. Many recipes in this book contain some form of milk as an ingredient. Should the milk listed in the recipe be not of your choosing, please feel free to substitute the same amount of the milk you prefer.

HOW MUCH PROTEIN DO I NEED?

According to the USDA, most people need approximately **0.4 grams of protein per pound of body weight**. For example, if you weigh 150 pounds, you would need about 60 grams of protein each day. For some people, this is not a difficult nutritional goal. However, for others, consuming this amount of protein could be somewhat challenging.

People who could benefit from additional protein:

- **Those trying to lose weight.** If you have begun your weight-loss journey, adding extra protein to your diet will help you feel fuller and more satiated, especially if you are trying to reduce refined carbohydrates and sugar. Researchers suggest increasing your protein intake to 0.7 grams per pound of body weight.

- **Those who are over sixty.** Increasing your protein intake to 0.6 grams per pound of body weight will help protect your body from sarcopenia, which is age-related muscle loss.

- **Advanced athletes.** These people are looking to add muscle mass to their body to perform at peak levels. Increasing protein up to 0.8 grams per pound of body weight will help build additional muscle mass. This protein recommendation is for those who are exercising daily for multiple hours at a time and looking to gain muscle mass. If you're like most of us who exercise for an hour or so, three days a week, this recommendation is not for you.

- **Women who are pregnant or nursing.** Obviously, women who are pregnant or nursing will have different nutritional and protein needs; they are amazingly growing another human with their body! If you are pregnant or nursing, be sure to consult your OBGYN as to exactly how much protein you need in your diet. Your specific pregnancy, along with age and personal health, will determine what you should be consuming.

SWEETENERS

All the recipes in this book have been tested for the best and most optimal taste and sweetness. These smoothies primary rely on the sweetness from the fruits, vegetables, juices, and milks that are added. However, should you prefer a slightly sweeter smoothie, here are some great options to add to your drink:

HONEY

Honey is one of nature's best sweeteners. A 1-tablespoon serving of honey contains 60 calories and around 17 grams of sugar. Add judiciously, perhaps starting with 1 teaspoon, as this natural sweetener can quickly overpower your smoothie.

STEVIA EXTRACT

This natural sweetener is derived from the stevia leaf. Because it is 200 to 350 times sweeter than sugar, only 0.1 gram of stevia is in a single packet of stevia sweetener. A ½ teaspoon serving of stevia contains 0 calories and less than 0.5 grams of sugar. A little bit of this sweetener goes a long way, but it's a fantastic choice when trying to avoid calories and sugar.

AGAVE NECTAR

This sweetener looks and tastes like honey but is derived from the succulent plant, blue agave. Agave is a great natural option for sweetness, as it has a low glycemic index. There are 60 calories in 1 tablespoon of agave nectar and 14 grams of sugar.

MEDJOOL DATES

Dates are a good option, especially if you're looking to add more volume to your smoothie in addition to sweetness. Medjool dates are golden in color and often have the pit remaining, which will need to be removed prior to blending into your smoothie. Dates also offer a low glycemic index and have some nutritional benefits, including minerals like phosphorous, calcium, potassium, and magnesium. Dates are more caloric, as one serving (4 medium dates) contains approximately 280 calories and 66 grams of sugar. Start with one date, and blend as needed.

SELECTING PRODUCE

Often, selecting fruits and vegetables is as simple as heading to your local grocery store or market. Is it that simple? Here's what you need to know to get the best quality produce for your money.

1. **Whenever you can, shop locally**. Shopping your local farmers' market or farm stand will pretty much always land you superior quality produce. Not only will it be at its peak freshness, you can be assured it didn't spend half of its shelf life on a truck or in a warehouse. When you purchase your produce locally, you're also helping support your local farmers, community, and economy.

2. **Whenever you can, purchase organic produce**. I realize that organic produce is not readily accessible to the masses. Nor is it a good economical choice for many people. However, if you can find it, and can afford it, purchase organic. The Environmental Working Group (EWG) releases an annual list of the "Dirty Dozen." These are the top twelve fruits and vegetables containing the most contamination by pesticides and chemicals.

   Here's a recent list of the top twelve most pesticide-contaminated fruits and vegetables according to the EWG. Whenever you can, try to purchase these organically, and check the EWG's website yearly to find out what has changed.

   1 Strawberries
   2 Spinach
   3 Nectarines
   4 Apples
   5 Grapes
   6 Peaches
   7 Cherries
   8 Pears
   9 Tomatoes
   10 Celery
   11 Potatoes
   12 Sweet Bell Peppers

3. Whenever you can, choose fresh produce at its peak season. You'll find the best quality fruits and vegetables at the best price.

   If you're looking for produce that is out-of-season (like strawberries in November or peaches in April), your next best option is heading to the freezer section at your grocery store. Frozen fruit is typically picked at its peak freshness, then flash-frozen and packaged.

   You can also freeze your own produce. Purchasing produce in bulk while in its peak season is a great way to capture the freshest fruits to use later when they may not be as accessible. Page 13 shows you how to easily do it at home.

THE TOOLS YOU'LL NEED

Making your own smoothies will require minimal tools—likely items you already have and regularly use in your kitchen.

Here's what you'll need:

- Measuring cups and spoons:
    - Clear, glass measuring cups are ideal for measuring liquids.
    - Dry measuring cups are ideal for chopped fruits and veggies, nuts, and yogurts.
    - Measuring spoons will be useful for nut butters, spices, and ground or shredded foods.
- Knives:
    - A simple paring knife is essential for removing stems and peels and cutting many fruits and vegetables.
    - A medium serrated utility knife is always a helpful tool in the kitchen. This is helpful in slicing melons and cutting through citrus fruits.
    - A large serrated knife with a long blade is ideal in removing skins and rinds of pineapple and melons.

HOW TO FREEZE FRESH PRODUCE

Start by placing fresh, clean fruit on a sheet pan lined with parchment or waxed paper. This will ensure the fruit does not freeze to the pan. Fruit needs to be in a single layer, not overlapping or stacked on top of each other. Place the pan of fruit in the freezer until completely frozen.

This is the ideal way to freeze bananas. Peel and slice the bananas and place in a single layer. Each row represents one banana. Place the pan in the freezer until the banana slices are completely frozen. Each row (banana) can then be bagged into individual or snack-sized resealable freezer bags for storage.

Using resealable plastic freezer bags are a great option for freezing and storing fresh fruit. Many of the recipes in this book call for a single frozen banana. Having these individual frozen bananas pre-portioned and frozen are very convenient and will save time when blending. You can also pre-portion your berries or any other frozen fruit you wish.

- An all-purpose cutting board. You will use this often, so select a board that is easy to clean and store and is large enough to accommodate most fruits and vegetables.
- A blender. This is an essential tool in making smoothies.

In development and testing of the recipes in this book, we used two models. Both models are excellent tools to blend smoothies and are great overall appliances to add to your kitchen. Here are the pros and cons for each machine that we noted:

The Vitamix Professional 750 Series Blender

Pros: This blender had a very powerful motor and was superb in achieving the best, most smooth puree.

Cons: It had a bit of trouble when trying to break up large pieces of frozen fruits. This is noted in the user's manual. Adding extra liquid helped this process.

The Nutri Ninja Professional 1500W Blender System:

Pros: This blender comes equipped with a taller, multi-level stacked blade. This made it very quick to break apart frozen fruits.

Cons: It was more difficult for this blender to achieve a truly smooth puree when greens were added to the smoothie. Blending the liquid and greens first, prior to adding any other ingredients, helped alleviate this issue.

1. Start with greens

2. Next, add liquid

3. Next, fresh fruit

4. Next, yogurts or nut butters

5. Next, powders, nuts, or seeds

6. Lastly, frozen fruits or veggies

Erin Indahl-Fink

BEST BLENDER TECHNIQUES

In recipe development and testing, we discovered that the order of ingredients when placed in the blender is helpful in achieving the best and smoothest puree of ingredients.

1. Start with any greens, like kale or spinach, that are noted in the recipe.
2. Next, add any liquids like milks, juices, or waters.
3. Next, add any fresh, unfrozen fruits or vegetables.
4. Next, and any yogurts or nut butters.
5. Next, add any powders, nuts, seeds, or spices.
6. Lastly, add any frozen fruits or vegetables.

We discovered that this order of ingredients, when placed in the blender, helped aid the blade viscosity, achieving the best possible puree.

Additional note: Should your blender leave you with chunks of greens, begin by blending the greens and liquid first. Once these are adequately blended, then add the remaining ingredients.

Do you have a single-serve cup blender? If so, reverse the order of ingredients added to the cup. Since the cup is inverted when placed on the blender, the liquids and soft items will need to be closest to the blade. Here is the order you will need for a single-serve blender cup:

1. Start with any frozen fruits or vegetables.
2. Next, add any powders, nuts, seeds, or spices.
3. Next, and any yogurts or nut butters.
4. Next, add any fresh, unfrozen fruits or vegetables.
5. Next, add any liquids like milks, juices, or waters.
6. Lastly, add any greens, like kale or spinach, that are noted in the recipe.

Chapter 2
Breakfast Blends

Blending up a delicious breakfast smoothie is the perfect way to get your day off to a healthy start. For many of us, morning is a rushed, hectic time, especially when there are kids in the mix. Here's the good news; blending up a delicious, protein-rich smoothie takes just five minutes or less.

These recipes are designed to be easy to make, and loaded with healthy ingredients, great for boosting much-needed energy in the morning, fueling your body and keeping you full well into lunchtime.

Raspberry Rise & Shine

This fruity, delicious blend is the perfect way to start your day! Loaded with antioxidants, potassium, calcium, and protein, this breakfast smoothie will be one of your favorites.

Serves: 1 medium (8 oz.) smoothie

½ cup cran-raspberry juice, or similar juice
⅔ cup vanilla Greek yogurt
¼ cup whole, raw almonds
1 frozen banana
½ cup frozen raspberries

Add all ingredients into blender, and blend until smooth. If using fresh instead of frozen raspberries, consider adding ½ to 1 cup of ice to thicken to your desired consistency. Enjoy right away while cold.

Blueberry Oatmeal

Flavorful and filling, this delicious breakfast smoothie will get your day off to a great start. Enjoy as a smoothie bowl, and top with additional blueberries and oats, or pour into a travel mug for a breakfast on the go.

Serves: 1 large (16 oz.) smoothie or 2 small (8 oz.) smoothies

¾ cup almond milk

½ cup plain Greek yogurt

¼ cup old-fashioned oats, dry

1 cup frozen blueberries

1 frozen banana

Optional sweeteners: 1 teaspoon of stevia, agave nectar, or honey

Add all ingredients into blender, and blend until smooth. If you would prefer this smoothie with additional sweetness, consider adding stevia, agave nectar, or honey. Enjoy right away while cold.

Chai Spice Iced Latte

Forget the long line at the coffee shop, this creamy, delicious smoothie is a healthier way to enjoy your favorite chai. Blended with all your favorite spices, the flavor of this smoothie is spot on!

Serves: 1 medium (8 oz.) smoothie

½ cup almond milk
½ cup vanilla Greek yogurt
⅛ teaspoon cinnamon
⅛ teaspoon allspice
⅛ teaspoon cloves
⅛ teaspoon ginger
1 frozen banana

Add all ingredients into blender, and blend until smooth. Enjoy right away while cold.

Peanut Butter Banana Oatmeal

Grab a spoon and dig in! This ultra-creamy, delicious smoothie bowl will be your new favorite brekkie. Loaded with protein and packed with flavor, this smoothie will keep you full well into lunchtime!

Serves: 1 large (16 oz.) smoothie or 2 small (8 oz.) smoothies

½ cup almond milk
½ cup vanilla Greek yogurt
2 tablespoons natural peanut butter
¼ cup old-fashioned oats, dry
1 frozen banana

Add all ingredients into blender, and blend until smooth. Top with additional banana slices, and/or chopped peanuts, if desired. Enjoy right away while cold.

Strawberry Citrus Sunrise

The perfect fresh, fruity flavors that will have you looking forward to breakfast before you go to bed! Loaded with vitamin C, this is also the perfect smoothie to protect your immune system during cold and flu season.

Serves: 1 medium (8 oz.) smoothie

½ cup vanilla Green yogurt
1 orange, peeled and seeded
½ cup frozen strawberries
1 frozen banana

Add all ingredients into blender, and blend until smooth. If using fresh strawberries, consider adding ½ cup ice. Enjoy right away while cold.

Turning Health into a Verb

Health isn't just a condition or state of being; it's also a state of mind. Making the conscious decision to make healthier food choices requires action. It involves making the choice—the movement, the momentum—to put good quality food into your body.

Healthy isn't just food; it is activity, motion, moving your body. A body in motion stays in motion—that is real! Move your body and what happens can be life-changing. You will look better, feel better, and honestly, be more pleasant to be around.

Healthy is a choice. Just like happiness, healthy is a conscious decision. The path to health requires putting one foot in front of the other; it requires you to act! To do! No one is going to do it for you. There is only one you, and you were given only one body. How you choose to treat it will literally determine the outcome of your life. You are the only person who can take that step. If you want to be healthy, if you want to be happy, then act. Do. Health is a verb.

Chocolate Almond Croissant

Skip all the extra fat and empty calories in the traditional bakery-style croissant and enjoy this amazing smoothie instead! With the chocolate and almond flavors that you're craving, along with protein, potassium, vitamins and minerals that your body needs, this protein smoothie is the perfect swap for a croissant.

Serves: 1 medium (8 oz.) smoothie

½ cup almond milk
1 tablespoon almond butter
2 medjool dates, pits removed
1 scoop chocolate protein powder
1 frozen banana

Add all ingredients into blender, and blend until smooth. Enjoy right away while cold.

Pumpkin Spice Latte

Did you know the average coffee shop PSL contains nearly 400 calories and 14 grams of sugar? Instead, save yourself some money and calories, and make yourself a healthier, more filling version! This Pumpkin Spice Latte smoothie has all the spicy, fall flavors that you love and includes protein and vitamins as well. A much smarter way to do the PSL!

Serves: 1 large (16 oz.) smoothie or 2 small (8 oz.) smoothies

½ cup almond milk
½ cup vanilla Greek yogurt
¼ teaspoon pumpkin pie spice
½ teaspoon stevia sweetener
½ cup frozen coffee cubes (approximately 4 cubes)
½ cup frozen pumpkin puree (approximately 4 pumpkin cubes)

Add all ingredients into blender, and blend until smooth. Enjoy right away while cold.

Mocha Lovers

A coffee shop mocha is often loaded with sugar and calories. Instead, make a healthier swap in this Mocha Lovers smoothie! With all your favorite chocolate and coffee flavors, this healthier smoothie will have you skipping the coffee shop all together.

Serves: 1 medium (8 oz.) smoothie

½ cup almond milk
1 scoop chocolate protein
4–6 frozen coffee cubes
1 frozen banana
Optional: cacao nibs for topping

Add all ingredients into blender, and blend until smooth. Enjoy right away while cold.

Chapter 3
Fruity Favorites

Flavor and freshness take center stage in these fruit-filled favorites! Designed to introduce amazing flavor combinations, these fruity protein smoothies are simple to make for a breakfast, snack, or post-workout recovery drink.

Many of us are not getting our recommended daily servings of fruit in any given day. Blending up one of these fruit smoothies will add valuable vitamins and minerals that have vast health benefits. Your body will thank you!

Mango Peach

This smoothie has a wonderfully creamy, light consistency. With three servings of fruit, this smoothie will provide your body with vitamins and minerals to fuel you and energize your day.

Serves: 1 large (16 oz.) smoothie or 2 small (8 oz.) smoothies

¾ cup coconut milk
1 medium peach, with or without the skin
½ cup plain Greek yogurt
1 cup frozen mango
1 frozen banana

Add all ingredients into blender, and blend until smooth. Enjoy right away while cold.

Piña Colada

Many restaurants and bars serve up a piña colada that contains nearly 500 to 600 calories a drink! Who needs all those calories and sugar when you can make this healthy alternative for your own personal happy hour? Tastes amazing and will have you dreaming of the beach!

Serves: 1 large (16 oz.) smoothie or 2 small (8 oz.) smoothies

½ cup coconut milk

Juice of ½ lime

½ cup coconut Greek yogurt

¼ cup unsweetened coconut flakes or coconut meat

1 cup frozen pineapple

Add all ingredients into blender, and blend until smooth. Enjoy right away while cold.

Tropical Passion

The flavor and aroma of this delicious smoothie will have you thinking of a tropical island vacation! Loaded with lots of vitamin C, as well as protein and fiber, it's also the perfect breakfast drink or afternoon snack.

Serves: 1 large (16 oz.) smoothie or 2 small (8 oz.) smoothies

¼ cup coconut milk

½ cup coconut Greek yogurt

½ cup mango

¼ cup unsweetened coconut flakes or coconut meat

1 cup frozen pineapple

Add all ingredients into blender, and blend until smooth. Enjoy right away while cold.

Blueberry Coconut

This creamy, thick smoothie will keep you full for hours! The blueberries and coconut are the perfect flavor combination, and great with a sprinkle of your favorite granola for a tasty breakfast.

Serves: 1 large (16 oz.) smoothie or 2 small (8 oz.) smoothies

1 cup coconut milk

¼ cup unsweetened coconut flakes or coconut meat

1 scoop vanilla protein powder

1 cup frozen blueberries

Add all ingredients into blender, and blend until smooth. Enjoy right away while cold.

Very Cherry & Red Raspberry

A popular family favorite! This smoothie has great cherry flavor, which makes it perfect for a quick, healthy breakfast or a tasty afternoon snack.

Serves: 1 large (16 oz.) smoothie or 2 small (8 oz.) smoothies

¼ cup cran-cherry juice, or similar juice
⅓ cup almond milk
½ cup plain Greek yogurt
1 cup frozen raspberries
½ cup fresh or frozen cherries

Add all ingredients into blender, and blend until smooth. Enjoy right away while cold.

Watermelon Margarita

With many restaurant-style margaritas topping out at more than 500 calories a glass, this simple, delicious mocktail is a smart swap. A fantastic way to do cocktail hour without all the sugar and calories!

Serves: 1 large (16 oz.) smoothie or 2 small (8 oz.) smoothies

Juice of 1 lime
2 cups seedless watermelon
Zest of 1 lime
1 teaspoon agave nectar
1 scoop vanilla protein

Add all ingredients into blender, and blend until smooth. Enjoy right away while cold.

Cherry Strawberry Bliss

With two full servings of fruit, you'll be well on your way to a healthy, energized day. Sweet and creamy, this healthy smoothie is loaded with vitamins and antioxidants! Your body will thank you!

Serves: 1 large (16 oz.) smoothie or 2 small (8 oz.) smoothies

1 cup almond milk
1 scoop vanilla protein powder
½ cup frozen cherries
1 frozen banana
1 cup frozen strawberries

Add all ingredients into blender, and blend until smooth. Enjoy right away while cold.

Apple, Kiwi & Melon

Fantastic fruity freshness, this healthy smoothie will be your new favorite midday snack. Loaded with vitamin C, this smoothie is a great way to boost your immune system to help you stay healthy and energized!

Serves: 1 large (16 oz.) smoothie or 2 small (8 oz.) smoothies

1 cup honeydew melon

1 kiwi, peeled

1 medium apple, peeled and cored

½ cup vanilla Greek yogurt

Optional: for additional protein, add 1 scoop of vanilla protein powder

For best results with this smoothie, choose a sweeter variety apple like Fuji, Red Delicious, Pink Lady, or Honey Crisp. Add all ingredients into blender, and blend until smooth. Enjoy right away while cold.

Berry Beet Blend

This incredibly flavorful and filling smoothie will keep you coming back for more! When paired with blueberries and blackberries, this berry and beet blend takes on additional anti-inflammatory properties, providing you with an incredibly healthy way to fuel your body!

Serves: 1 medium (8 oz.) smoothie

½ cup cherry juice
½ cup beets, steamed and cooled
½ cup plain Greek yogurt
½ cup fresh or frozen blueberries
¼ cup fresh or frozen blackberries
Optional: sweetener of choice

Add all ingredients into blender, and blend until smooth. If using fresh blueberries and blackberries, consider adding ½ to 1 cup of ice. Pour into glass, and top with additional fresh berries, if desired. Enjoy right away while cold.

Spiced Apple & Butternut Squash

Enjoy those delicious, spicy fall flavors any time of year with this delightful veggie smoothie! Packed with vitamins C, E, and B_6, this nutritional powerhouse is perfect for protecting your immune system and fighting off sickness.

Serves: 1 medium (8 oz.) smoothie

¼ cup almond milk

½ cup butternut squash, steamed and cooled

1 medium apple, peeled and cored

½ cup vanilla Greek yogurt

⅛ teaspoon cinnamon

⅛ teaspoon nutmeg

For best results, choose a sweet variety apple like Fuji, Red Delicious, Pink Lady, or Honey Crisp.

Add all ingredients into blender, and blend until smooth. Enjoy right away while cold. Feel free to use fresh or frozen butternut squash (if out of season).

Pear & Carrot Twist

The nutritional benefits are vast in this delicious veggie smoothie! Carrots are a great source of several vitamins and minerals, and when "paired" with a sweet, juicy pear, you're left with a smoothie that will power your body and energize your day!

Serves: 1 large (16 oz.) smoothie or 2 small (8 oz.) smoothies

1 pear, peeled and cored
1 cup carrots, steamed and cooled
½ cup plain Greek yogurt
⅛ teaspoon fresh ginger, grated

Add all ingredients into blender, and blend until smooth. Enjoy right away while cold.

Wishing versus Working

It is simply not enough to wish for health or to hope it happens. At some point, we need to realize that time is going to pass regardless. We must be willing to work for what we desire in that given time. No one is going to give it to us. No one else will want your dream of being healthy as much as you do. That dream belongs to you, but only if you are willing to work for it. You must take immediate action and put in the hard work to make that dream a reality. Not tomorrow, not next week, not at the beginning of the new year. You need to take action now.

Wishing for something to happen is for suckers. Working for something to happen is for achievers. Be an achiever.

Sweet Potato & Mango Medley

A.k.a. the Fountain of Youth smoothie, it's loaded with vitamins A and C, which help prevent premature aging, promote skin health, and ward off degenerative disease. Drink up, and glow from the inside out!

Serves: 1 medium (8 oz.) smoothie

½ cup coconut milk

1 medium sweet potato, peeled, cooked, and cooled (about ⅔ cup)

¼ teaspoon allspice

¼ teaspoon cinnamon

1 scoop vanilla protein powder

½ cup frozen mango

Add all ingredients into blender, and blend until smooth. Enjoy right away while cold. If using fresh mango, consider adding extra ice to thicken.

Chapter 4
Green Machine

Green smoothies are one of the best ways to add some serious nutrition to your body. Superfoods like kale, spinach, and avocado are packed with some of the best antioxidants, anti-inflammatory components, vitamins, and minerals. When these foods are paired with fruits like citrus, pineapple, melon, apples, and berries, they take on some wonderful flavors.

Making one of these nutritionally rich green protein smoothies is the perfect addition to any healthy way of living. As an amazing breakfast, healthy snack, or light lunch, these blends will power your body and keep you energized.

Apple Spinach Sensation

The adage of "an apple a day keeps the doctor away" is especially true with this smoothie! When paired with the super-foods spinach and avocado, this smoothie will not only keep the doctor away, but will help you thrive!

Serves: 1 medium (8 oz.) smoothie

½ cup coconut water
1 cup fresh baby spinach (1 big handful)
1 medium apple, peeled and cored
½ avocado
1 teaspoon fresh grated ginger
1 scoop vanilla protein

For best results, choose a sweeter variety apple like Fuji, Red Delicious, Pink Lady, or Honey Crisp.

Add all ingredients into blender, and blend until smooth. Pour into glass, and top with additional apple slices, if desired. Enjoy right away while cold.

Melon & Mint

The amazing flavors of summer pop in this protein smoothie! Made with honeydew and cantaloupe along with fresh mint leaves, this refreshing drink is the perfect way to energize your body.

Serves: 1 large (16 oz.) smoothie or 2 small (8 oz.) smoothies

¼ cup coconut milk
1 cup honeydew melon
1 cup cantaloupe
3–4 fresh mint leaves
1 cup fresh baby spinach (1 big handful)
1 scoop vanilla protein powder

Add all ingredients into blender, and blend until smooth. Enjoy right away while cold.

The Perfect Pear

Green grapes, spinach, banana, and pear are a match made in smoothie heaven! This naturally sweet smoothie is loaded with potassium, flavonoids, and fiber, making it the perfect breakfast or post-workout smoothie. It's the perfect way to refuel your body and get your day off to a great start!

Serves: 1 large (16 oz.) smoothie or 2 small (8 oz.) smoothies

½ cup coconut milk
1 cup fresh baby spinach (1 big handful)
1 cup green grapes
1 fresh, ripe pear (any variety), peeled
½ cup vanilla Greek yogurt
1 banana, frozen

Add all ingredients into blender, and blend until smooth. Pour into glass, and top with additional grapes and pears, if desired. Enjoy right away while cold.

Mango Mojito

Forget the bar scene, this fantastic mocktail is perfect for kicking back after a long day. Made with fresh baby kale, mint, and mango, this refreshing smoothie will help aid in immune and digestive health and slow the aging process.

Serves: 1 large (16 oz.) smoothie or 2 small (8 oz.) smoothies

1 cup coconut water
Juice of ½ lime
1 cup fresh baby kale, stems removed
3–4 fresh mint leaves
1 scoop vanilla protein powder
1 cup frozen mango

Add all ingredients into blender, and blend until smooth. Enjoy right away while cold.

Peachy Keen

Peaches and spinach come together for a winning combination! This healthy protein smoothie is one that will also energize your body and keep you feeling your best.

Serves: 1 medium (8 oz.) smoothie

1 cup fresh baby spinach (1 big handful)
½ cup orange juice
½ cup vanilla Greek yogurt
1 cup fresh or frozen peaches
1 frozen banana

Add all ingredients into blender, and blend until smooth. Enjoy right away while cold.

Find Your People

Healthy involves having the right people in your life. Toxic people are detrimental to your health and state of being. Toxicity is contagious. Start hanging out with people who are working toward the same goals you are.

Find people who are positive. Find the people who radiate good energy, have faith in something greater than themselves, and who encourage and inspire. Find the doers, the go-getters, people who are continuously looking for better ways of health, balance, and well-being. These are the people you want on your team. These are the people who will lift you up, instead of complaining, criticizing, or try to pull you back into the complacency you're desperately trying to escape.

Find your people, and you will find healthy.

Pineapple Power

This amazing protein smoothie is perfect after a long workout, hike, or run! Pineapple has anti-inflammatory components, which help reduce inflammation in joints and muscles. Your body will thank you!

Serves: 1 medium (8 oz.) smoothie

1 cup fresh baby spinach (1 big handful)
½ cup coconut milk
½ cup coconut Greek yogurt
½ cup frozen pineapple
1 frozen banana

Add all ingredients into blender, and blend until smooth. Enjoy right away while cold.

Kiwi Honeydew

Those little kiwis pack a serious nutritional punch! Just one kiwi contains your full daily dose of vitamin C, which helps boost your immune system. When paired with spinach, this delicious, refreshing smoothie will help keep you healthy and thriving!

Serves: 1 medium (8 oz.) smoothie

1 cup fresh baby spinach (1 big handful)
1 cup honeydew melon
1 fresh kiwi, peeled
1 scoop vanilla protein powder
1 frozen banana

Add all ingredients into blender, and blend until smooth. Enjoy right away while cold.

Berry Avocado

The perfect creamy, filling breakfast or lunch that will keep you full for hours. Loaded with vitamins and minerals and packed with flavor, this healthy protein smoothie is the perfect way to energize your day!

Serves: 1 medium (8 oz.) smoothie

½ cup coconut milk
½ avocado
1 scoop vanilla protein powder
1 banana, frozen
½ cup frozen strawberries

Add all ingredients into blender, and blend until smooth. Enjoy right away while cold.

Bloody Mary Mocktail

An amazing brunch mocktail when you don't want all that extra stuff! Blend up this delicious smoothie and reap the rewards of vitamins A and C, fiber, and of course, protein. The ultimate savory smoothie!

Serves: 1 medium (8 oz.) smoothie

1 (5.5 oz.) can, tomato juice
1 cup baby kale
½ red bell pepper
¼ cup chopped celery
¼ teaspoon salt
1 scoop <u>unflavored</u> collagen protein
Optional: a few shakes of hot sauce and/ or Worcestershire sauce

Add all ingredients into blender, and blend until smooth. Enjoy right away while cold.

Avocado Lovers

One amazing nutrient-dense smoothie that happens to taste incredible! Loaded with multiple vitamins and minerals, this delicious veggie smoothie is an amazing way to start your day.

Serves: 1 large (16 oz.) smoothie or 2 small (8 oz.) smoothies

½ cup almond milk
1 cup fresh baby spinach (1 big handful)
½ avocado
½ cup peeled cucumber
¼ cup whole, raw almonds
1 scoop vanilla protein
½ cup frozen pineapple

Add all ingredients into blender, and blend until smooth. Enjoy right away while cold.

Cucumber Honeydew

Fresh, light, and delicious, this veggie smoothie is the perfect, nutrient-dense drink! Fantastic for fighting inflammation, improving digestion, and detoxification, this will be your new favorite healthy snack.

Serves: 1 large (16 oz.) smoothie or 2 small (8 oz.) smoothies

Juice of ½ lime
1 cup fresh honeydew melon
1 cup fresh baby spinach (1 big handful)
½ cup fresh cucumber, peeled
½ cup vanilla Greek yogurt
¼ cup whole, raw almonds
2 tablespoons flaxseed

Add all ingredients into blender, and blend until smooth. Enjoy right away while cold.

Inner Peas

Fresh, creamy, and loaded with nutrition! This healthy vegetable smoothie contains key ingredients to fighting disease and strengthening immunity. The ultimate drink for cold and flu season!

Serves: 1 large (16 oz.) smoothie or 2 small (8 oz.) smoothies

¼ cup orange juice
1 orange, peeled and seeded
1 cup fresh baby spinach (1 big handful)
½ cup green peas, cooked and cooled
½ cup plain Greek yogurt
½ cup frozen pineapple

Add all ingredients into blender, and blend until smooth. Enjoy right away while cold.

Chapter 5
Road to Recovery

Any exercise physiologist will tell you that the key to peak athletic performance has just as much to do with how you fuel your body as how many reps you do or how many minutes of cardio you can endure. Successful athletic performance relies heavily on exactly what you're putting into your body, and specifically how well you recover from training and performance.

The protein smoothies in this chapter were specifically designed to offer maximum nutrition and anti-inflammatory components to athletes at all levels. Foods that fight inflammation, like berries, citrus, beets, pineapple, spinach, avocados, nuts, and seeds all take center stage in these recipes. Whether you exercise a few times a week, or every day, these smoothies will be your new favorite way to keep your body performing at its best.

Citus Sensation

Loaded with vitamin C and potassium, this uber-healthy protein smoothie will keep you at the top of your game. These vitamins and minerals will also aid in bone and muscle health.

Serves: 1 medium (8 oz.) smoothie

¼ cup coconut milk
1 orange, peeled and seeded
1 tangerine, peeled and seeded
¼ teaspoon orange zest
1 scoop vanilla protein powder
1 frozen banana

Add all ingredients into blender, and blend until smooth. Enjoy right away while cold.

Green Kiwi Cooler

As an athlete, avocado, kiwi, and pineapple are some of the best foods you can put in your body! Loaded with antioxidants, these fruits will help heal and restore joints and muscles. This smoothie is the ultimate fit fuel!

Serves: 1 medium (8 oz.) smoothie

½ cup coconut milk

1 kiwi, peeled

½ avocado

1 tablespoon chia seeds

1 scoop vanilla pea protein powder

1 cup frozen pineapple

Add all ingredients into blender, and blend until smooth. Enjoy right away while cold.

Pineapple Avocado Winner

This delicious green smoothie will be your new favorite way to refuel and recover after a tough workout! Made with pineapple, avocado, spinach, and banana, this recovery drink is loaded with potassium, iron, and anti-inflammatory bromelain. Sore muscles don't have a chance when armed with this nutrient-dense smoothie!

½ cup coconut water
1 cup fresh baby spinach (1 big handful)
½ avocado
1 scoop vanilla plant-based protein powder
½ cup frozen pineapple
1 frozen banana

Add all ingredients into blender, and blend until smooth. Pour into glass, and top with additional fresh pineapple or banana slices, if desired. Enjoy right away while cold.

Berry Good Recovery

Fantastic as a post-workout recovery drink, this hearty, delicious smoothie will restore your energy! Loaded with anti-inflammatory ingredients, this smoothie will benefit sore muscles and will help you refuel for your next workout.

Serves: 1 medium (8 oz.) smoothie

½ cup almond milk
¼ cup whole, raw almonds
1 scoop vanilla plant-based protein powder
½ cup frozen blueberries
½ cup frozen cherries
¼ cup frozen blackberries

Add all ingredients into blender, and blend until smooth. Enjoy right away while cold.

Apple Cherry Almond

This healthy, nutritious smoothie tastes just as good as it looks. Loaded with vitamin C and antioxidants, this smoothie will help aid in joint and muscle health, keeping you in peak physical condition.

Serves: 1 medium (8 oz.) smoothie

½ cup almond milk
½ cup plain Greek yogurt
1 medium apple, peeled and cored
¼ cup whole, raw almonds
½ cup frozen cherries

For best results choose a sweeter variety apple like Fuji, Red Delicious, Pink Lady, or Honey Crisp. Add all ingredients into blender, and blend until smooth. Enjoy right away while cold.

Peach Powerhouse

Loaded with protein and packed with favor, this healthy protein smoothie will keep you in peak performance mode! Feel free to use fresh peaches if they're in season or go for frozen for quick convenience.

Serves: 1 medium (8 oz.) smoothie

¾ cup almond milk
¼ teaspoon fresh grated ginger
¼ cup whole, raw almonds
1 scoop vanilla plant-based protein powder
1 cup frozen peaches

Add all ingredients into blender, and blend until smooth. Enjoy right away while cold.

Mango Beet

With beets and mango, this uber-nutritious smoothie will have you looking and feeling your best! Loaded with vitamins C, A, and B$_6$, this protein smoothie will boost your immune system and keep you at the top of your game!

Serves: 1 medium (8 oz.) smoothie

½ cup orange juice
½ cup beets, steamed and cooled
¼ teaspoon fresh grated ginger
1 scoop <u>unflavored</u> collagen protein powder
½ cup frozen mango

Add all ingredients into blender, and blend until smooth. Enjoy right away while cold.

Blueberry Almond Chia

Between the anti-inflammatory and healing properties of chia seeds and blueberries in this protein smoothie, you'll be ready for your next sweat session! These healthy ingredients are exactly what your body needs when recovering from multiple workouts.

Serves: 1 large (16 oz.) smoothie or 2 small (8 oz.) smoothies

½ cup almond milk
1 cup plain Greek yogurt
1 tablespoon chia seeds
¼ cup whole, raw almonds
1 cup frozen blueberries

Add all ingrdients into blender, and blend until smooth. Enjoy right away while cold.

Chapter 6
Meal Replacement

Many of us find ourselves overscheduled and rushed for time to eat during the day. Often, we end up skipping meals, which usually has disastrous after-effects, such as headaches, fatigue, and poor food choices later in the day. Planning ahead and taking five minutes to make one of these delicious, filling meal-replacement protein smoothies is the perfect solution to our busy lives.

Designed to offer ample amounts of fiber and protein, these smoothies will be slightly more caloric than others in this book. Using the best possible ingredients, these smoothies will help satiate our appetite and keep us feeling fuller. This can also help alleviate unnecessary snacking. These smoothies will also offer fruits and vegetables, providing us with optimum nutrition while doing everything from boosting our immune systems to fighting off disease. The perfect healthy way to enjoy a meal on the go!

Triple Berry Chiller

Loaded with blueberries, strawberries, and raspberries, this berry protein smoothie is the ultimate meal in a glass! Containing valuable vitamins, dietary fiber, and flavonoids, these berries, along with the chia seeds and protein, will give you a boost of energy and keep you going all day long!

Serves: 1 large (16 oz.) smoothie or 2 small (8 oz.) smoothies

1 cup almond milk
1 tablespoon chia seeds
1 scoop vanilla protein powder
½ cup fresh or frozen blueberries
½ cup fresh or frozen strawerries
½ cup fresh or frozen raspberries

Add all ingredients into blender, and blend until smooth. If using fresh berries, add ½ to 1 cup of ice to thicken the smoothie. Pour into glass, and top with additional fresh berries, if desired. Enjoy right away while cold.

Tropical Island

Healthy, flavorful, and filling, this delicious meal-replacement smoothie will power your day! This smoothie contains loads of protein and fiber to stave off hunger and keep you focused and productive.

Serves: 1 medium (8 oz.) smoothie

¾ cup coconut milk

¼ cup unsweetened flake coconut or coconut meat

1 scoop vanilla protein powder

½ cup frozen pineapple

½ cup fresh or frozen mango

Add all ingredients into blender, and blend until smooth. Enjoy right away while cold.

Almond Vanilla

One of our very favorite smoothies during testing! With ingredients designed to help stave off hunger and keep you full for hours, this nutritious protein smoothie will help energize your day!

Serves: 1 medium (8 oz.) smoothie

¼ cup almond milk
½ cup vanilla Greek yogurt
2 tablespoons almond butter
1 scoop vanilla protein powder
1 frozen banana

Add all ingredients into blender, and blend until smooth. Enjoy right away while cold.

The Choice of Moving Forward

The choice and conscious decision of moving forward is difficult but must happen for us to have healthy lives and relationships. Moving forward means you make the decision to leave behind the baggage that you've been carrying. Everything that has happened in the past cannot be changed. We cannot let our regrets and our failures, or the trauma that we've endured, dictate our future. Instead, let us use those failures as opportunities to learn, be better, be focused on the real, true things in our life.

We must take accountability for the mistakes we've made. Stop playing the victim. Once you make the choice to own your mistakes and failures, it will no longer have a hold on your life. You will be set free.

Healthy means moving forward and accepting ourselves for exactly who we are—mistakes, flaws, and everything in between. For in acceptance, comes clarity, and with clarity we finally see everything that we are made of and what we're capable of achieving.

Moving forward may just be the greatest gift we can ever give ourselves in leading our healthiest, truest lives.

Pumpkin Power

This delicious pumpkin smoothie is the ultimate healthy alternative to the over-sugared, heavy Pumpkin Spice Latte. Loaded with vitamins and minerals, this protein smoothie will energize you for hours!

Serves: 1 medium (8 oz.) smoothie

½ cup almond milk
½ cup vanilla Greek yogurt
1 tablespoon flaxseed
¼ teaspoon pumpkin pie spice
½ cup frozen pumpkin puree (4 frozen pumpkin cubes)
1 frozen banana
Optional: frozen coffee cubes

Add all ingredients into blender, and blend until smooth. Enjoy right away while cold.

Cinnamon Apple Spice

With wonderful apple cinnamon flavors, this highly nutritious protein smoothie is an excellent breakfast or light lunch option. The perfect flavors of fall!

Serves: 1 medium (8 oz.) smoothie

¼ cup cashew milk
½ cup vanilla Greek yogurt
1 medium apple, peeled and cored
2 tablespoons cashew butter
⅛ teaspoon cinnamon
Optional: cup of ice to thicken

Add all ingredients into blender, and blend until smooth. Enjoy right away while cold.

Green Citrus

The ultimate protein smoothie, perfect for breakfast or lunch on-the-go! Loaded with vitamins A, C, and E, along with protein and iron, this delicious drink will help energize and fuel your body with superfood-fueled nutrition.

Serves: 1 large (16 oz.) smoothie or 2 small (8 oz.) smoothies

¼ cup orange juice

1 cup fresh baby spinach (1 big handful)

1 orange, peeled and seeded

½ cup plain Greek yogurt

½ cup frozen pineapple

Optional: if looking for additional protein, add 1 scoop of the protein powder of your choice

Add all ingredients into blender, and blend until smooth. Enjoy right away while cold.

Chocolate Almond Coconut

Craving chocolate? The flavor and thickness in this delicious chocolate protein smoothie are incredible. Designed to help keep you full for hours, this protein smoothie is the perfect excuse to have chocolate for breakfast or lunch!

Serves: 1 medium (8 oz.) smoothie

½ cup almond milk
⅓ cup unsweetened coconut flakes or coconut meat
2 tablespoons almond butter
1 scoop chocolate protein powder
1 frozen banana

Add all ingredients into blender, and blend until smooth. Enjoy right away while cold.

Strawberries & Cream

Thick, creamy, and loaded with vitamin C, this delicious smoothie will help boost your immune system and fuel your body with the nutrition it needs. Perfect for a light breakfast or lunch on the go!

Serves: 1 medium (8 oz.) smoothie

½ cup almond milk
½ cup vanilla Greek yogurt
1 tablespoon chia seeds
1 scoop vanilla protein powder
1 cup frozen strawberries

Add all ingredients into blender, and blend until smooth. If using fresh berries, add ½ to 1 cup of ice to thicken the smoothie. Pour into glass, and top with additional fresh berries, if desired. Enjoy right away while cold.

Chapter 7
Decadent Dessert Blends

Are desserts and sweet treats your weakness? For many of us, desserts are our downfall. The good news is, we don't have to deprive ourselves to stay healthy. In fact, indulging in a sweet, healthy alternative is a great way to satiate that craving and feel satisfied in the process.

These sweet protein smoothies were designed with the dessert lover in mind. Each of these smoothies is a healthy alternative to the overly decadent traditional dessert that it is named after. Not only designed to save you calories, these smoothies are a nice way to add some nutrition to our bodies in the process.

Bananas Foster

This creamy, delicious banana smoothie is the perfect alternative to the heavier, calorie-laden dessert. Bananas along with medjool dates paired with vanilla Greek yogurt give this smoothie a wonderfully creamy, sweet consistency that tastes amazing!

Serves: 1 medium (8 oz.) smoothie

¼ cup almond milk
½ cup vanilla Greek yogurt
¼ teaspoon cinnamon
2 medjool dates, pits removed
1 frozen banana
Optional toppings: low-fat whipped cream topping and/or low-sugar caramel sauce (ice cream topping)

Add all ingredients into blender, and blend until smooth. Pour into glass, and top with whipped cream and caramel drizzle, if desired. Enjoy right away while cold.

Carrot Cake

Did you know that a slice of carrot cake can exceed 1,000 calories? Make the swap with this delicious, nutritionally rich smoothie that has all the same flavors of the heavy cake. Your body will thank you!

Serves: 1 large (16 oz.) smoothie or 2 medium (8 oz.) smoothies

½ cup coconut milk

½ cup carrots, steamed and cooled

½ cup vanilla Greek yogurt

¼ cup unsweetened flake coconut or coconut meat

⅛ teaspoon cinnamon

⅛ teaspoon nutmeg

½ cup frozen pineapple

1 frozen banana

Optional toppings: walnuts and/or unsweetened flake coconut

Add all ingredients into blender, and blend until smooth. Enjoy right away while cold.

Coconut Cream Pie

Cool, creamy, and loaded with delicious coconut flavor, this protein smoothie is the perfect healthy option to the overly sugary dessert. For another option, freeze this smoothie and enjoy as "nice cream," which you can eat with a spoon!

Serves: 1 medium (8 oz.) smoothie

½ cup coconut milk
⅛ teaspoon coconut extract
⅔ cup vanilla Greek yogurt
½ cup unsweetened flake coconut or coconut meat
Optional toppings: low-fat whipped cream and/or unsweetened flake coconut

Add all ingredients into blender, and blend until smooth. Top with whipped cream, if desired. Enjoy right away while cold.

Strawberry Shortcake

This creamy, delicious strawberry smoothie is the perfect alternative to the heavier, calorie-laden shortcake. The strawberries paired with the vanilla Greek yogurt give this smoothie the perfect creamy consistency that tastes amazing!

Serves: 1 medium (8 oz.) smoothie

⅔ cup coconut milk
½ cup vanilla Greek yogurt
1 scoop vanilla protein powder
1 cup frozen strawberries
Optional topping: low-fat whipped cream topping

Add all ingredients into blender, and blend until smooth. If using fresh strawberries, add ½ to 1 cup of ice to thicken the smoothie. Pour into glass, and top with whipped cream, if desired. Enjoy right away while cold.

Mint Chocolate Chip

If mint chocolate chip ice cream is one of your favorite treats, then this healthier protein smoothie will be right up your alley! With all the same amazing minty flavors, this smoothie is the perfect alternative to all the sugar and unhealthy fats in bowl of ice cream.

Serves: 1 medium (8 oz.) smoothie

½ cup almond milk
⅛ teaspoon peppermint extract
1 scoop chocolate protein powder
1 frozen banana
Optional topping: 2 teaspoons mini chocolate chips

Add all ingredients into blender, and blend until smooth. Top with mini chocolate chips, if desired. Enjoy right away while cold.

Peanut Butter Brownie

Creamy, delicious, and much healthier than a sugary, overly heavy bakery brownie. This delicious chocolate protein smoothie is a fantastic snack when your chocolate cravings hit!

Serves: 1 medium (8 oz.) smoothie

¾ cup almond milk
2 tablespoons powdered peanut butter
1 scoop chocolate protein powder
1 frozen banana

Add all ingrediets into blender, and blend until smooth. Enjoy right away while cold.

Pumpkin Pie

The traditional Thanksgiving dinner dessert has met its match with this flavorful, delicious smoothie! With natural sweetness from medjool dates, and the pumpkin spice flavor, you'll enjoy every sip of this healthy protein smoothie!

Serves: 1 medium (8 oz.) smoothie

½ cup almond milk
½ cup vanilla Greek yogurt
2 medjool dates, pits removed
¼ teaspoon pumpkin pie spice
½ cup frozen pumpkin puree (4 pumpkin cubes)

Add all ingredients into blender, and blend until smooth. Enjoy right away while cold.

Chocolate-Covered Cherry

If your chocolate cravings are about to get the best of you, reach for this simple, delicious protein smoothie! Perfect for blending as an after-dinner treat or a midday snack.

Serves: 1 medium (8 oz.) smoothie

½ cup almond milk
1 scoop chocolate protein powder
1 cup frozen cherries

Add all igredients into blender, and blend until smooth. Enjoy right away while cold.

The Art of Hustle

Don't just hustle for the sake of hustling. We live in a society that glorifies "busy," yet at the end of the day we often feel like we've accomplished nothing. Hustle should require forethought. It should be intentional, focused, and directly related to our big goals.

Sometimes it feels like we need to be better "multi-taskers." Don't be fooled—multitasking is a myth. If someone tells you they are a great multi-tasker, it only means they are great at getting lots of things unfinished, and nothing completely done. Hustle doesn't mean multi-task fast. It means picking a worthwhile task and focusing solely on it for as long as you can. It's purposeful, intentional, and will help you get just a little bit better every day.

Be real with yourself about hustle. Be honest with your purpose and why you do it. Dig deep about why you are hustling. Put your energy and intent on what means the most to you, and you'll achieve your greatest goals.

Chapter 8
Kids in the Kitchen

Kids might be the biggest smoothie fans of us all! The little people in our lives are on to something when it comes to enjoying fun, creamy breakfasts and snacks. Now it's their turn to get in the kitchen and help blend up their favorite treats! With recipes built to use simple ingredients and offer the best possible nutrition their growing bodies need, these smoothies will make fantastic choices as after-school snacks or breakfasts for busy mornings.

These kid-friendly smoothie recipes are the perfect way to get our kids interested and involved in helping create their favorite blends. These easy recipes were developed to help kids learn how to chop, measure, and blend up their favorite drinks. When we get our kids involved in the process of making what they eat, they will be much more interested in making healthy food choices. A win-win!

Chunky Monkey

Bananas and peanut butter are the perfect combination in this delicious protein smoothie! A great on-the-go breakfast for a busy school day, you can feel good knowing your kids had a healthy start to their day.

Serves: 1 medium (8 oz.) smoothie

¼ cup almond milk
½ cup vanilla Greek yogurt
2 tablespoons natural peanut butter
1 frozen banana

Add all ingredients into blender, and blend until smooth. Enjoy right away while cold.

Climbing a Mountain

Do you have a mountain to climb? Is there a goal or dream in your life that you want terribly, but it feels completely out of reach?

Sometimes we feel that if we just had enough willpower, work hard enough, hustle fast enough, or want it bad enough that we can turn our dreams into reality. For some this may be true. But when that big goal or finish line is so far out of reach, that we can barely see it, our vision gets blurred. Sometimes we get so tired of hustling or frustrated that we're not getting there fast enough that we lose sight of our real, true goal.

Challenge yourself to be just a little bit better every day. If we can pick one small thing to accomplish in one day, and achieve it, we are moving forward. Chip away, bit by bit. Keep your focus and know that it's okay to fall once in a while. Stay the course. That rock will turn into a boulder, and that boulder then becomes the mountain.

Watermelon Razzle

Fun and fruity, this delicious protein smoothie makes for a fantastic after-school snack. Loaded with vitamins and minerals, this healthy smoothie is no match for the prepackaged, processed snack foods.

Serves: 1 large (16 oz.) smoothie or 2 small (8 oz.) smoothies

¼ cup coconut milk
2 cups seedless watermelon
¾ cup vanilla Greek yogurt
½ cup frozen raspberries

Add all ingredients into blender, and blend until smooth. To thicken, add ½ to 1 cup of ice. Enjoy right away while cold.

Crisscross Applesauce

If your kids love apples and applesauce, this yummy protein smoothie will be right up their alley! Perfect for an easy breakfast or a satisfying after-school snack, this smoothie will have your kids jumping for joy.

Serves: 1 medium (8 oz.) smoothie

½ cup natural apple juice
1 medium apple, peeled and cored
½ cup vanilla Greek yogurt
1 teaspoon honey
¼ teaspoon cinnamon
1 frozen banana
Ice, to thicken

For best results, choose a sweeter variety apple like Fuji, Red Delicious, Pink Lady, or Honey Crisp. Add all ingredients into blender, and blend until smooth. Add ice to thicken, if necessary. Enjoy right away while cold.

Grape Ape

The pretty purple color of this smoothie will have your kids in awe! With red and green grapes, along with blueberries, this tasty smoothie is loaded with nutrition to help fuel their growing bodies.

Serves: 1 large (16 oz.) smoothie or 2 medium (8 oz.) smoothies

½ cup coconut milk
1 cup red and green grapes
½ cup vanilla Greek yogurt
½ cup frozen blueberries
1 frozen banana

Add all ingredients into blender, and blend until smooth. Enjoy right away while cold.

Triple Berry Blastoff

The perfect way to answer the "I'm hungry" snack attacks! This uber-healthy smoothie is the perfect way to stave off midday hunger and keep your kids fueled for fun activities or after-school sports.

Serves: 1 large (16 oz.) smoothie or 2 small (8 oz.) smoothies

⅔ cup coconut milk
1 scoop vanilla protein powder
½ cup frozen strawberries
½ cup frozen blueberries
½ cup frozen raspberries
1 frozen banana

Add all ingredients into blender, and blend until smooth. Enjoy right away while cold.

Frozen Strawberry Lemonade

If your kids love a good glass of lemonade, why not turn it into a healthy snack? Loaded with vitamin C and protein, this is a great option for protecting your kids' immune systems during cold and flu season.

Serves: 1 medium (8 oz.) smoothie

½ cup natural lemonade
Juice of ½ lemon
½ cup vanilla Greek yogurt
1 cup frozen strawberries
1 cup ice

Add all ingredients into blender, and blend until smooth. Enjoy right away while cold.

Orange Creamsicle

Forget the ice cream truck and the over-sugary popsicles—this delicious smoothie gets all its flavor and sweetness from real fruit. Perfect for blending up and enjoying as an after-school snack or an after-dinner treat.

Serves: 1 large (16 oz.) smoothie or 2 medium (8 oz.) smoothies

¼ cup orange juice
1 orange, peeled and seeded
½ cup vanilla Greek yogurt
1 cup frozen peaches
1 frozen banana

Add all ingredients into blender, and blend until smooth. Enjoy right away while cold.

Chocolate Peanut Butter Buddy

Who needs the candy aisle? Your kids will adore this tasty chocolate peanut butter smoothie! With all the same amazing flavors as their favorite candy, this smoothie is a fantastic healthy option when they want a sweet dessert.

Serves: 1 medium (8 oz.) smoothie

½ cup almond milk
2 tablespoons powdered peanut butter
¼ cup vanilla Greek yogurt
1 scoop chocolate protein powder
1 frozen banana

Add all ingredients into blender, and blend until smooth. Enjoy right away while cold.

Acknowledgments

First and foremost, I want to thank my husband, Jason, and my son, Harrison. The both of you sacrificed quite a bit for me to take on this project. No vacations or trips to the beach, just photos of smoothies and work. Thank you for being so flexible, understanding, supportive, and resilient through this entire process. I am so grateful for you and love you with all my heart. You guys are the best thing that ever happened to me.

To my dear friend and production assistant, Sarah Griffith; I am so incredibly blessed and grateful to have such a great friend like you in my life. Not only did you help keep us on track with testing and photography, but you cleaned up messes, washed countless dishes, and kept us laughing through the whole thing. You made writing this book fun and something that I will remember for the rest of my life.

To my parents, Deb and Blue Indahl. Thank you for teaching me how to make my way around a kitchen. Thank you for getting me involved in 4-H as a kid, where I not only learned how to cook, bake, and sew but also learned how to use a camera. You taught me that creativity and being unique is a good thing, and that being just like the rest of the kids is boring. Most of all, thank you for loving me for exactly who I am.

To my OTF family, thank you for choking down countless smoothies. Every single one of you are inspiring, supportive, and encouraging. I think of you as my tribe and extended family. You challenge me to be just a little bit better every single day, and for that I am incredibly grateful. I am truly blessed to be a part of such an amazing group of people.

Lastly, thank you to the good people at Skyhorse Publishing, especially Nicole Frail. Thank you for taking a chance on me and offering to fulfill a dream. Your hard work, patience, knowledge, and attention to detail brought this dream to life. I am incredibly appreciative of this opportunity that you brought my way.

About the Author

Erin Indahl-Fink is a food blogger, writer, and photographer living in Northern Virginia. She is the author and founder of the successful blog *Delightful E Made*, an online resource that provides easy and delicious recipes for every home cook. Erin takes pride in writing recipes that not only inspire people to cook, but to also make food that brings friends and family closer together.

Erin's work has been featured in numerous online publications, including *Buzzfeed*, *Huffington Post*, *Redbook*, *Country Living*, *Self*, *Fitness*, *Women's Day*, and *Today Food*.

Erin was born and raised in the "small-but-mighty" rural farm town of Burke, South Dakota. Being the oldest of four children, Erin quickly learned how to cook and bake at a young age—not out of curiosity, but because of necessity. At the age of eight, she became involved in 4-H and honed her skills as a cook, baker, and photographer.

After graduating high school, Erin went on to the University of South Dakota, where she received her bachelor's in business management from the USD School of Business. She then went on to work in sales and marketing, as well as project management in the tech industry.

After college, Erin resided in Boise, Idaho, where she then met her husband, Jason. Jason and Erin have one son, Harrison, and they now reside in Manassas, Virginia.

You can find Erin on Instagram, Facebook, Pinterest, and Twitter @delightfulemade. Please come over, say hello, and check out all of her delicious creations!

Index

Conversion Charts

Metric and Imperial Conversions

(These conversions are rounded for convenience)

Ingredient	Cups/Tablespoons/ Teaspoons	Ounces	Grams/Milliliters
Fruit, dried	1 cup	4 ounces	120 grams
Fruits or veggies, chopped	1 cup	5 to 7 ounces	145 to 200 grams
Fruits or veggies, puréed	1 cup	8.5 ounces	245 grams
Honey, maple syrup, or corn syrup	1 tablespoon	0.75 ounce	20 grams
Liquids: cream, milk, water, or juice	1 cup	8 fluid ounces	240 milliliters
Salt	1 teaspoon	0.2 ounces	6 grams
Spices: cinnamon, cloves, ginger, or nutmeg (ground)	1 teaspoon	0.2 ounce	5 milliliters
Sugar, brown, firmly packed	1 cup	7 ounces	200 grams
Sugar, white	1 cup/ 1 tablespoon	7 ounces/0.5 ounce	200 grams/12.5 grams
Vanilla extract	1 teaspoon	0.2 ounce	4 grams

Liquids

8 fluid ounces = 1 cup = ½ pint
16 fluid ounces = 2 cups = 1 pint
32 fluid ounces = 4 cups = 1 quart
128 fluid ounces = 16 cups = 1 gallon